Samuel French Acting Edition

Omnium Gatherum

by Theresa Rebeck &
Alexandra Gersten-Vassilaros

SAMUELFRENCH.COM   SAMUELFRENCH.CO.UK

Copyright © 2004 by Madwoman in the Attic, Inc.
and Alexandra Gersten-Vassilaros
All Rights Reserved

OMNIUM GATHERUM is fully protected under the copyright laws of the United States of America, the British Commonwealth, including Canada, and all other countries of the Copyright Union. All rights, including professional and amateur stage productions, recitation, lecturing, public reading, motion picture, radio broadcasting, television and the rights of translation into foreign languages are strictly reserved.

ISBN 978-0-573-62959-4

www.SamuelFrench.com
www.SamuelFrench.co.uk

For Production Enquiries

United States and Canada
Info@SamuelFrench.com
1-866-598-8449

United Kingdom and Europe
Plays@SamuelFrench.co.uk
020-7255-4302

Each title is subject to availability from Samuel French, depending upon country of performance. Please be aware that *OMNIUM GATHERUM* may not be licensed by Samuel French in your territory. Professional and amateur producers should contact the nearest Samuel French office or licensing partner to verify availability.

CAUTION: Professional and amateur producers are hereby warned that *OMNIUM GATHERUM* is subject to a licensing fee. Publication of this play(s) does not imply availability for performance. Both amateurs and professionals considering a production are strongly advised to apply to Samuel French before starting rehearsals, advertising, or booking a theatre. A licensing fee must be paid whether the title(s) is presented for charity or gain and whether or not admission is charged. Professional/Stock licensing fees are quoted upon application to Samuel French.

No one shall make any changes in this title(s) for the purpose of production. No part of this book may be reproduced, stored in a retrieval system, or transmitted in any form, by any means, now known or yet to be invented, including mechanical, electronic, photocopying, recording, videotaping, or otherwise, without the prior written permission of the publisher. No one shall upload this title(s), or part of this title(s), to any social media websites.

For all enquiries regarding motion picture, television, and other media rights, please contact Samuel French.

MUSIC USE NOTE

Licensees are solely responsible for obtaining formal written permission from copyright owners to use copyrighted music in the performance of this play and are strongly cautioned to do so. If no such permission is obtained by the licensee, then the licensee must use only original music that the licensee owns and controls. Licensees are solely responsible and liable for all music clearances and shall indemnify the copyright owners of the play(s) and their licensing agent, Samuel French, against any costs, expenses, losses and liabilities arising from the use of music by licensees. Please contact the appropriate music licensing authority in your territory for the rights to any incidental music.

IMPORTANT BILLING AND CREDIT REQUIREMENTS

If you have obtained performance rights to this title, please refer to your licensing agreement for important billing and credit requirements.

actors theatre of louisville **PRESENTS**
27th Annual Humana Festival of New American Plays
made possible by a generous grant from The Humana Foundation

Omnium Gatherum

march **02** - april **06, 2003**

by **ALEXANDRA GERSTEN-VASSILAROS** and
THERESA REBECK
directed by **WILL FREARS**

THE CAST

Suzie	**KRISTINE NIELSEN***
Roger	**PHILLIP CLARK***
Lydia	**ROMA MAFFIA***
Julia	**MELANNA GRAY***
Khalid	**EDWARD A. HAJJ***
Terence	**DEAN NOLEN***
Jeff	**RICHARD FURLONG†**
Mohammed	**JAY CHARAN***

Setting: An elegant dinner party.
Time: The present, or somewhere around there.

Scenic Designer	**PAUL OWEN**
Costume Designer	**LORRAINE VENBERG**
Lighting Designer	**TONY PENNA**
Sound Designer	**VINCENT OLIVIERI**
Properties Designer	**MARK WALSTON**
Stage Manager	**KATHY PREHER***
Production Assistant	**JUSTIN McDANIEL**
Fight Director	**BRENT LANGDON**
Dramaturg	**SARAH GUBBINS**
Casting	**ORPHEUS GROUP CASTING**
	with special assistance from **BILLY HOPKINS**
Directing Assistant	**DEVON HIGBY**

*Member of Actors' Equity Association, the union of professional actors and stage managers of the United States
† Member of Actors Theatre's Apprentice Company

Presented by special arrangement with
International Creative Management, Inc. and The Joyce Ketay Agency

Omnium-Gatherum was first read at Actors Studio, New York City, March 2002
Developed at New York Stage and Film Company and The Powerhouse Theatre at Vassar College in July 2002
Workshopped at Naked Angels, New York City, January 2003
China provided courtesy of Lenox, Incorporated.
Food preparation generously donated by the Seelbach-Hilton.

VARIETY ARTS THEATRE
Under the direction of BEN SPRECHER and WILLIAM P. MILLER

ROBERT COLE JOYCE JOHNSON

IN ASSOCIATION WITH

JUJAMCYN THEATERS CHARLES FLATEMAN/KERRIN BEHREND

PRESENT

OMNIUM GATHERUM

BY

THERESA REBECK ALEXANDRA GERSTEN-VASSILAROS

STARRING

AMIR ARISON JENNY BACON PHILLIP CLARK MELANNA GRAY
EDWARD A. HAJJ KRISTINE NIELSEN DEAN NOLEN JOSEPH LYLE TAYLOR

SET DESIGN
DAVID ROCKWELL

COSTUME DESIGN
JUNGHYUN GEORGIA LEE

LIGHTING DESIGN
JULES FISHER & PEGGY EISENHAUER

SOUND DESIGN
VINCENT OLIVIERI

CASTING
BERNARD TELSEY CASTING

TECHNICAL SUPERVISION
GENE O'DONOVAN

PRODUCTION STAGE MANAGER
JANE GREY

PRESS REPRESENTATIVE
RICHARD KORNBERG & ASSOCIATES

GENERAL MANAGER
LISA M. POYER

DIRECTED BY
WILL FREARS

PREMIERED IN THE 2003 HUMANA FESTIVAL OF NEW AMERICAN PLAYS AT ACTORS THEATRE OF LOUISVILLE
THE PRODUCERS WISH TO EXPRESS THEIR APPRECIATION TO THEATRE DEVELOPMENT FUND FOR ITS SUPPORT OF THIS PRODUCTION

*To our husbands,
Jess Lynn and John Vassilaros,
co-dependents and co-conspirators*

CHARACTERS

Suzie
Roger
Lydia
Julia
Khalid
Terence
Jeff
Mohammed

SETTING

An elegant dinner party

TIME

The present, or somewhere around there

(A beautifully set table dominates the room. There is a chandelier overhead. Everyone is seated and quickly ending a lively conversation about rhubarb.)

TERENCE. *(Declaring.)* Rhubarb.
JULIA. *(Agreeing.)* Rhubarb.
JEFF. I love rhubarb.
SUZIE. No, it's a moody fruit. You can only use it in combination. Go on, Khalid.
KHALID. As I was saying—If we could but shrink the earth's population to a village of precisely 100 people—
ROGER. Oh, no. Is this that?
LYDIA. Let him finish.
KHALID. With the existing human ratios—
ROGER. *(Overlap.)* We all got this on the internet!
TERENCE. *(Overlap.)* I didn't!
KHALID. Oh—perhaps, then, if people already know—
TERENCE. I don't!
SUZIE. *(Overlap.)* No no, we're listening, recap, recap—

(She goes around the table, placing little plates with tiny silver bubbles on them before all her guests.)

KHALID. All right then. Simply: there would be 57 Asians, 21 Europeans—

SUZIE. *(To TERENCE, overlap.)* Don't peek—
TERENCE. *(Overlap.)* But I am anxious, desperate anxious—
KHALID. 14 from the Western Hemisphere, both north and south, 8 Africans—
SUZIE. *(Overlap.)* This is very important what he's saying, it's absolutely the right place to start—
KHALID. 52 would be female—
LYDIA. A majority, ha ha ha ha!
SUZIE. *(Setting down a bubble.)* Amuze bouche, to amuse your mouth!
KHALID. 48 would be male. 70 would be non-white.
SUZIE. Non-white, meaning—?
JULIA. Uh. Not, uh, white.
SUZIE. *(Laughs.)* Oh I see, of course, go on!

(She laughs, JULIA laughs, and then everyone laughs.)

KHALID. 70 would be non-Christian. 30 would be Christian. 89 would be heterosexual, 11 would be homosexual.
SUZIE. Stop that. I'll tell you when you can look.

(SUZIE slaps TERENCE's hand, as he tries to peek.)

KHALID. Shall I keep going?
SUZIE. Yes yes, we're fascinated.
KHALID. 6 people would possess 59% of the entire world's wealth and all 6 would be from the United States.
JULIA. Oh, my dear god. That's horrifying.
ROGER. Not to me.
KHALID. 80 would live in substandard housing. 70 would be unable to read. 50 would suffer from malnutrition.
SUZIE. *(Clanging on a little triangle.)* Could I interrupt for a moment. Merely a taste treat, *(A very bad French accent.)* a "pre-appetizer," ladies and gentlemen—you may lift your thingies!

(They lift the silver hoods and on everyone's plate is a very tiny portion of something.)

    JULIA. My oh my. It's the size of a jelly bean.
    ROGER. What is it?
    TERENCE. Where is it?
    JEFF. Wow. It's pretty small.
    SUZIE. Pre-appetizer, to prepare and stimulate the palate!
    TERENCE. Ah, then it's not food, exactly, it's preparation for food.
    SUZIE. It's a marvelous mini sweet potato scotch bonnet raviolini thingiedo, with a spoonful of chanterelle—not yet, Terence!—mushroom sauce, garnished with fresh cilantro shoots.
    JULIA. *(A gasp.)* Oh my.
    SUZIE. Carry on, with your list, Khalid, dear.
    KHALID. *(As everyone eats.)* There's not much more to it. One would be near death.
    JEFF. This is—amazing.
    TERENCE. Oh my gracious—
    ROGER. Whoa—Suz—

(All are moaning with delight at the taste of the thing.)

    KHALID. One would be near birth.
    LYDIA. *(A shout of delight.)* Ohhh! This is unbelievable.
    KHALID. Only one would have a college education. One! When you consider our world from such a compressed perspective, the need for acceptance and understanding is so urgent, my friends. So urgent.
    JEFF. Can I ask for another?
    TERENCE. Me too!
    SUZIE. Only one per person. Don't worry. There's food aplenty. I'll be right back.

(SUZIE disappears into a smoking red hole in the ground. ROGER

stands up, startled.)

JEFF. I think that was good, but there was so little of it it's kinda hard to tell.

ROGER. Whoa! What the hell is that?

JULIA. I'm resisting the urge to lick the plate.

ROGER. Suz? Suzie? Sukie, honey? Anybody else see that?

SUZIE. *(Reentering from trap door, holding a bottle up as she enters.)* Cheers! Everyone! I nearly forgot! Ta ta ta ta!!! This is an exquisite Tenuta dell Ornellai-ay-ay-ay from the house of Something, the year, let's see, squinting, squinting, nineteen hundred and eighty-five.

TERENCE. Pass it down, dear, I'll do the honors.

SUZIE. Yes, please, unleash the elixir! I was feeling so badly after the attacks I bid on two cases of this stuff.

(TERENCE starts to uncork two bottles while SUZIE puts several others on the sideboard.)

KHALID. Another example of the unquestioning American drive for acquisition.

ROGER. Don't knock capitalism. That's the only way this country will recover. Get the money flowing. Create wealth.

SUZIE. No that's not what I was doing, I was just thinking about getting a little tipsy with my favorite people.

TERENCE. Ah, the bouquet, it's exquisite. How much was this?

JULIA. Is there anybody else who is worried by that, the idea that our spiritual response to any catastrophe should be to go out and shop?

ROGER. No, it's a good idea. I'll be damned if I'd spend my money on French wine, but—

SUZIE. Okay, you can just drink it then. There's nothing wrong with a little retail therapy, is there, Khalid?

KHALID. I have reservations but perhaps I've already said too

much.
TERENCE. There he goes, down into his own little existential hell.
SUZIE. Already?
TERENCE. Don't worry, he comes right out. I've known him for years. It's the discrepancies he finds so howlingly alarming. *(Holding up his glass.)* Cheers, mates! Here's to discrepancies! *Le monde se lon l'homme!*
JULIA. I'd like to bless the meal.
SUZIE. *(Surprised.)* Oh!

(JULIA stands, lowers her head, and prays. Everyone follows suit.)

JULIA. We have come together tonight in the hope of understanding and fellowship. Suzie has generously shared her gifts with us by creating this beautiful feast, a plenty of nourishment for our souls and our bodies. We thank her for that. Bless this food. Bless this moment, and everyone here. Bless the life that fills this room, and holds us in harmony with the living universe. Amen.
ALL. Amen.
SUZIE. Thank you, Julia. That was lovely.
TERENCE. *(Any chance to celebrate.)* Splendid! Hear hear!
KHALID. Yes, very beautiful sentiment to be sure.
SUZIE. And now it's time for the first course!

(A tray full of food suddenly appears in a doorway.)

LYDIA. I'm starved.
JEFF. Me too.
SUZIE. This is a beautiful wild salmon, caught in the deep waters of the Columbia River, which has been assiduously rubbed with rock salt and exotic Spanish spices, pan-roasted and ingeniously served on a tower of sliced ruby crescent fingerlings. *(Plainly, to ROGER who doesn't get it.)* Potatoes.
TERENCE. That's astonishing.

SUZIE. The whole meal has been designed by Bobby Flay. We go way back. Not as far back as some people— *(Off ROGER.)* But there was one night, in Santa Fe—oh, I can't tell you everything! This on the side, is a lovely warmish yellow pepper sauce with threads of saffron and young scallions.

LYDIA. In America, even our scallions are young.

(Everyone laughs, or tries to, at this terrible joke.)

SUZIE. *(Serving JEFF.)* Here you go, sweetheart.
JEFF. Thanks, Suzie.
SUZIE. *(To someone near.)* He's a fireman.
KHALID. Perhaps I might explain why that list was so provocative to me.
JEFF. Is there anything on tap?
SUZIE. We have imported water! Water pitcher! Could you pass this down, pass this down—

(She hands them water pitchers, which get passed down both sides of the table.)

KHALID. Unbridled capitalism has long been a concern to the global community—
SUZIE. *(To JULIA.)* I love your jacket, is that Donna's?
KHALID. Warnings have been made again and again and the resistance in America—
JULIA. I got it at Lohman's. They cut the tag out.
KHALID. —To the simplest examination of this basic question has been rather absolute. We must reflect.
LYDIA. Americans, reflect?
ROGER. Hey. You don't get to criticize us after you blew up the World Trade Center.

(They all protest at once.)

JULIA. He didn't—
JEFF. No, no, now—
SUZIE. Oh, no, we can't—
TERENCE. He didn't—
LYDIA. He didn't do it—
SUZIE. How can you say that?
JULIA. We have to be sensitive to racial issues.
ROGER. I'm not going to defend myself! I'm sorry, Suzie. I thought I was coming to a dinner party. I thought there would be a band or something, and now I'm stuck in the same old argument. People don't like capitalism, so lunatics get to come over here and blow things up? Sorry.
JULIA. I don't think that's what he—
ROGER. It makes me sick. Sukie. Let's put on some music, huh?
SUZIE. But we're debating!
ROGER. You can't debate with half-wits.

(JULIA, TERENCE and LYDIA protest this.)

KHALID. *(Overlap.)* You cannot just brush this away! These events cannot be seen as unrelated!
TERENCE. *(Overlap.)* Yes Khalid, but—lord I am loathe to second my conservative friend—
ROGER. Can I have the wine?
JULIA. Is there white? I don't want to overwhelm the salmon, it's exquisite by the way.
TERENCE. But you have to ask yourself—
SUZIE. White! Where is my head? Where is my head!!!?
TERENCE. Don't worry about it, Suzie dear, wild salmon stands up to red, it really does—
SUZIE. Oh dear, oh dear, oh dear!

(She rushes to the trap, opens it.)

TERENCE. *(Continuing.)* Suzie, really, darling—oh well.
KHALID. *(To TERENCE.)* Carry on.
TERENCE. As I was saying, Khalid, you must ask yourself if a causal relationship in this situation actually supports your thesis. *(SUZIE disappears in the trap. JULIA watches, fascinated.)* The proposition that mass murders committed by the most reactionary world actors are an expression of international outrage against the American marketplace, actually sabotages your argument in its nascency.
LYDIA. Whoa. What?
TERENCE. Cambridge, darling, you had to keep up. These men are madmen, you'd say they were psychotic, if that wasn't an insult to psychotics everywhere. If you link all critical analysis of the capitalist project to the destruction of the twin towers, you associate the horrific violence of one particular act with a much more benign set of goals—social justice, say, or the diminishment of poverty worldwide.
JULIA. They taught you that at Cambridge?
TERENCE. Yes, but what can you do with it, other than show off at dinner parties?
KHALID. I understand what you are saying—
JEFF. I don't.
KHALID. —But it is naive to ignore the fact that everywhere in the world this association is being made.

(SUZIE returns with many bottles.)

SUZIE. Here's the white! The white!! Roger, do the honors—

(She hands him a bottle.)

TERENCE. That doesn't stop it from presenting a version of reality which is every bit as mind-numbingly idiotic as everyone out there waving flags and saying God Bless America.
JEFF. I don't think that's idiotic.

TERENCE. Not idiotic then. Let's say unnerving.
LYDIA. Can I have the water, please?
SUZIE. Absolutely! Oh, you didn't eat your salmon.
LYDIA. I'm a vegan.
SUZIE. Oh. Oh—ah—I wish I had known that—
JEFF. Can I have your salmon, I mean, if you're not going to eat it?
LYDIA. Absolutely.
JEFF. This stuff is incredible. You should try it.
LYDIA. I can't.
TERENCE. What is a vegan? I mean, precisely?
LYDIA. I can't eat anything with a face.
JEFF. Fish don't have faces.
LYDIA. They most certainly do.
ROGER. Fish don't have beards.
TERENCE. They have faces but they don't have a nervous system.
JULIA. That's lobsters.
TERENCE. Lobsters and shellfish have ectoskeletons.
KHALID. Shells but no nervous systems.
LYDIA. *(Getting defensive.)* Then why do they scream when you put them in boiling water?
SUZIE. That's not the lobster, that's the steam that's trapped in the shell, dear.
LYDIA. How do you know?
SUZIE. I think I would know.
JULIA. I think he's right, I don't think fish have nervous systems either.
LYDIA. I don't care about the nervous system. I'm not eating anything with a face!
JULIA. Shellfish don't have faces.
LYDIA. Yes they do. Shrimp have eyes and tails.
TERENCE. Tails aren't faces.
LYDIA. I didn't say they were.
JEFF. Scallops! Scallops, clams and mussels have no faces.

ROGER. Scallops have faces. I had a pet scallop once.
SUZIE. Quahogs!
TERENCE. A quahog is a clam.
LYDIA. *(Finally.)* So, if this was a clam, I might eat it, but it's not a clam, it's salmon.
SUZIE. Do Arabs eat shellfish?
KHALID. I'll have to check my notes.
JEFF. Is there bread?
SUZIE. Oh no no. Bread is over!
JEFF. Over?
SUZIE. All that starch just interferes with the complexity of the meal. Besides, it's very bad for you.

(She slaps his hand.)

ROGER. Could I have the red, or is that your personal stash?
TERENCE. *(Lining up the bottles before him.)* I drink to make other people interesting.
JEFF. The white is really good.
JULIA. You know, a lot of times people in my congregation come to me, especially now, and they're feeling overwhelmed, and they want to know, What am I doing with my life? Is what I'm doing enough? I mean, when do we question our usefulness?
TERENCE. Never. Ever!
SUZIE. I'm useful! I've found a way to help women and men all over the world find their creative souls by embracing the domestic arts. I was just a caterer!
ROGER. *(Gracious and gruff.)* Suzie, there is nothing "just" about you. Then, or now.
SUZIE. Thank you, you old fatty. *(To others.)* We go way back.
JEFF. You started as a caterer?
SUZIE. Yes!
ROGER. She sure did!
SUZIE. I was working out of my basement! The immediate re-

sponse was terrific, well back then there weren't very many people doing it, word of mouth was really all you needed.

JULIA. How does that work? You go to people's houses and cook for them, or do you cook somewhere else and bring it—

SUZIE. That never works. Everything dries out.

ROGER. How about that catalogue food? Is that any good?

TERENCE. Exquisitely prepared filet mignon, just appearing at your doorstep, I confess I've fantasized about that.

JEFF. Those pictures, they look so delicious.

LYDIA. Can I just say that red meat from a catalogue sounds—

ROGER. Stop it right there, we're not interested.

SUZIE. No, don't do it. Catalogue food. Just don't do it.

JEFF. *(Prompting SUZIE.)* So the catering business took off.

SUZIE. Yes. And I realized—well, that people were looking for beauty in their lives. "Esthetic Serenity", I call it. And delicious food!

LYDIA. But this isn't like, spiritual. You know that, right?

SUZIE. No darling, really it is. That's what I'm saying.

ROGER. Don't criticize the hostess.

LYDIA. I wasn't criticizing, I was asking a question! You're the one, you were absolutely rude to me before—

SUZIE. A lively, contentious debate is the heart and soul of every dinner party but I do think we should wait until the main course is served, don't you? *(There is the loud sound of a helicopter passing overhead. They look up. Continuing; oblivious, to JEFF.)* Let me refresh your glass, dear. Anyone else?

(LYDIA holds her water glass up, as do several others. SUZIE pours.)

KHALID. I agree with Lydia.

LYDIA. How can you agree? I didn't get to finish my point.

ROGER. You implied. Your tone of voice—

LYDIA. My what?!?

KHALID. Suzie has had an entitled American experience. For you, this is a dream come true.

SUZIE. Oh yes!

KHALID. You pray at night and God answers your prayers, or seems to. Perhaps your secret terror is that it will vanish.

SUZIE. No.

KHALID. It will change.

SUZIE. No.

KHALID. You may have to share more.

SUZIE. *(Startled.)* Share more with whom?

(There is a slight, but deadly, pause. TERENCE clears his throat.)

TERENCE. Perhaps he's suggesting, and I hope you don't take it as an offense that I bring this up, but while you employ people all over the world, Suzie, and by the way, god this is monstrously good—

JULIA. Just delicious.

JEFF. I've never tasted anything ever I've liked so much.

(All demur.)

LYDIA. You were saying....

TERENCE. And I hope you don't think this is said in anything except the spirit of dinner party bonhomie, but the fact is—

ROGER. Can't you just get to the point?

TERENCE. Ah, but who can remember what it is?

(He laughs and reaches for the wine.)

LYDIA. Standard of living. That's where you're going.

TERENCE. Was I?

LYDIA. Weren't you?

TERENCE. They also taught discretion at Cambridge, darling.

SUZIE. No no, I want to know. What about my standard of living?

LYDIA. Not yours. The people who work for you.

SUZIE. What about them?
LYDIA. You don't pay them enough.
SUZIE. Oh, but I do. I'm sure I do.
LYDIA. How much do you pay them?
SUZIE. *(Suddenly forgetting.)* Pay who?
LYDIA. All the cookware and the kitchen mitts and the matching tablecloths and napkins and ironing boards have to come from somewhere, Suzie—

(SUZIE stands, annoyed, and passes around the salmon again.)

SUZIE. How could I keep all those facts and figures running through my head? I'd have to be a one man band. *(To JEFF.)* Would you like more? You worked so hard and we are so grateful for what you've done, have as much as you like.
JEFF. It's very good.
SUZIE. And so well mannered.

(She shoots LYDIA a look.)

JULIA. All the pieces of the puzzle are so complex.
KHALID. Yes, yes, it is overwhelming to even begin to approach—
ROGER. What are we supposed to do? Spend all our time worrying about the complexities? Listen to me. We don't have time. We're at war. So I'm not getting involved in all this hand-wringing. We have to get a little crazy on everybody, is what we have to do.
LYDIA. "Getting crazy on 'em," there's a sophisticated position.
ROGER. When they're getting crazy on us it's not time to be sophisticated!
SUZIE. *(Trying meekly to get attention.)* Um. Excuse me....
ROGER. I'm not arguing for over simplification, I'm just making it easy for the boob mentality.
LYDIA. "Boob" mentality?

JULIA. No, no. That's banal.

ROGER. "Banal?"

JULIA. The banal language of combat—I don't mean to insult, but—

ROGER. *(Overlap.)* There is what is right, and what is unfortunately necessary.

LYDIA. *(Overlap.)* No, no, she's right, that's just reductive and disgusting.

ROGER. *(Overlap.)* It's a code of war.

JULIA. Next thing you'll be saying "let's smoke 'em out—"

ROGER. Yes, and get 'em running—

SUZIE. *(Quietly.)* Pardone.

JULIA. Do you know what that is? That's the language of lynching. Do you even know that—

ROGER. You know that's not—

JULIA. Or Amos and Andy. Tonto and the Lone Ranger—

JEFF. Is there something wrong with them, too?

ROGER. No!

JULIA. Yes!

LYDIA. Yes! There is if that's what you think life is. That's what you think it all boils down to.

ROGER. *(Overlap.)* Don't pull that crap. I'm grateful that someone in this country is thinking about consequences. You should be too.

SUZIE. *(Hand raised.)* Excuse—

ROGER. Because if you don't like it here, if it's not evolved enough for you, find a better place! No I mean it!

LYDIA. *(Overlap.)* "Love it or leave it," it's the perfect answer to anyone suggesting we actually work at being a better nation—

ROGER. *(Overlap.)* Go to Baghdad. Go to Afghanistan for that matter, let the Taliban cover you in a sheet and throw you in an open grave for a couple weeks, then give me a call!

SUZIE. *(Finally!)* But what about me? What about my feelings? I mean, can I just say I feel a little itty bitty bit attacked? I appreciate what you're all saying but I do the best I can with what I have!! I give a heck of a lot of money away! I'm aware of my wealth. I used to be middle class. I know how that feels.

ROGER. *(Pointedly re: LYDIA.)* You're a nice person.

SUZIE. I'm trying. It's complicated. We're none of us, just one thing or another. Good or bad.

JULIA. You're right, Suzie. And that's why we fall into absolutism. Just pretending we're right and they're wrong, like there's security in that.

KHALID. So we are then, all of us seeking let's say, a false oneness to pull us through the demanding duality of life.

JULIA. Yes, it's so cunning how we do it. How we all judge and compare constantly.

TERENCE. But judgment is so relaxing. And fun!

JULIA. Yes, but it offers an utterly unreal feeling of power and security. And elitism. In fact, there's nothing real about it.

ROGER. There's nothing real in identifying an enemy?

JULIA. Enemy? See, that word is what I'm talking about—

ROGER. They're flying planes into buildings! What am I supposed to call them? What they did is pure evil! And I'm sick of hearing everyone make excuses!

JULIA. *(Overlap.)* "Evil," there's another one of those words.

ROGER. Oh, brother—

LYDIA. No, she's right. You all pull out words like "evil" to trick people into subscribing to your political agenda.

SUZIE. *(To JEFF.)* Do you need more white?

ROGER. Oh, so that's what I'm doing.

LYDIA. You're stealing from the Nazi playbook! They invented this kind of reckless dissemination of hysterical propaganda.

ROGER. Great, now I'm a Nazi.

TERENCE. I do think it was the Stalinists, darling—

SUZIE. White? White?

JULIA. Perhaps we should try to set reactivity aside, in our search for meaning.

SUZIE. White? White?

ROGER. She called me a Nazi!

JULIA. How do we stop arguing long enough to give ourselves half a second to find it?

SUZIE. Find what, I'm sorry?

TERENCE. Meaning dear. Meaning.

SUZIE. Ohhhhh.

ROGER. You think those Mullahs over there developing nuclear bombs and biological who-knows-what are looking for meaning?

LYDIA. *(Edgy.)* I think the point is that we should all be looking for meaning.

ROGER. You know, there's that tone again.

LYDIA. *(High, soft Marilyn voice.)* "Oh I'm sorry. Is this better?"

ROGER. Yes.

SUZIE. Try to get along! That's what Julia's saying! *(Taps her water glass aggressively.)* What can we agree on, that's the question!!

TERENCE. The wine is in my glass. The table is hard. The food is superb. Roger is an idiot. Sorry, sorry, just slipped out.

ROGER. I need a smoke.

LYDIA. No smoking!

SUZIE. *(Dinging glass.)* Agree! Agree!

ROGER. He called me an idiot!

KHALID. This reminds me of my childhood.

JULIA. We can agree that the food is delicious!

ROGER. Alright. Fine. Agreed.

JULIA. That we need the food—

SUZIE. We can agree on that, can't we?

LYDIA. I'm a vegan, so I actually do have issues here.

JULIA. You're a "vegan," but you need food.

LYDIA. Not meat! I don't need meat, and neither do you.

ROGER. I need meat, goddammit, it's protein. Only a fool doesn't eat protein.

LYDIA. But it's blood, you're eating blood!

TERENCE. *(Lifting his wineglass.)* Wine, the blood of you know who, does that count?

LYDIA. We don't need blood!
KHALID. Could you pass the wine?
ROGER. You're probably one of those Pita people.
LYDIA. Peta! Peta!
SUZIE. Bread is pita, this is Peta. Pita, Peta. Pita, Peta. Although all bread, as we know, is over!
ROGER. *(Re: LYDIA.)* Why is she here? I've spent my whole life trying to keep these people out of earshot.
SUZIE. It's a dinner party!
ROGER. Where's the music?
JULIA. This is the exercise. This is the meat of life.
TERENCE. Oh no, don't bring meat up again, please. Refills, anyone?

(He goes to the sideboard to open more wine. There is another sound of helicopters and explosions in the distance. People look around.)

SUZIE. Oh, I just wish that would stop!
KHALID. Do you know what it is?
SUZIE. No idea. None whatever.
JULIA. Is it something we should be worried about?
SUZIE. I certainly hope not.
JEFF. You want me to go look?
SUZIE. No, sit! Enjoy your meal!
ROGER. Here's what I have to say to all of you: JIHAD.
LYDIA. Meaning what?
ROGER. Meaning, look alive! You're talking about bread and meat and whatever—I wrote a huge bestseller about this!
SUZIE. *(Rising to escape Roger's story.)* Let me take that for you.
ROGER. And I mean, I won't go into the whole plot but—
JULIA. Can I give you a hand?
SUZIE. No, I'm fine.
ROGER. But after a catastrophic nuclear terrorist attack over in

another part of the world in Chapter One—
JULIA. Let me help you—
ROGER. It becomes obvious in Chapter Two, that the fate of the whole world can only be secure under the leadership of a kind of new world governance.
SUZIE. *(To JULIA.)* Don't forget the forks, dear.
ROGER. Which is run by, and here's where it gets interesting, the President of the United States of America of the World.
TERENCE. Oh bully for everyone!
ROGER. And by Chapter Four—
SUZIE. Uh huh. Listening. Listening.
LYDIA. May I have some red? Just a splash—
ROGER. No, no, I mean Chapter Six—
TERENCE. Take the white, the red is mine.
ROGER. A war begins between the International Terrorist Party and the M.I.E.C.
LYDIA. What's MIEC?
ROGER Military Industrial Entertainment Complex. Which is really the shadow government, see? With underground cities all over the world. And the Terrorist Party is trying to infiltrate it by having sex with—well, it's really a spy novel when you get down to it, but the point is, the point is …
TERENCE. Yessss.
ROGER. The point is that all the people, like you, had no goddamn imagination and then it happened! See, I wrote that years ago! I'm not just a good novelist, I'm fucking psychic!
TERENCE. Egads! Why didn't you call and warn them, man?
ROGER. You'll see. Ask him how it feels.

(He indicates JEFF. All eyes turn.)

JEFF. It feels ….

(After a moment, he shakes his head.)

ROGER. That's right. He can't even say. So do we have the right to stop them before they come at us again? You bet we do! Christ! If there's gonna be a goddamn world power, I'm glad it's us!

SUZIE. But why does there have to be a world power at all?

ROGER. Oh, grow up.

SUZIE. Rog!

ROGER. Oh. Sorry, Suz. It's just that if we let go of our power, someone else is just going to step up. And who is that going to be? Russia? China? Korea? *(To the others.)* See what I mean, see what I mean?

TERENCE. Another point, brilliantly made.

ROGER. Damn right. I need a smoke.

SUZIE. *(Clanging on the triangle.)* You don't have time for that! *(Another tray full of food appears.)* The main course *son't arrivez.* You're really going to enjoy this one! This, my friends, is a dish from the south of Pakistan, a favorite among moderate Shiite's— *(To ROGER.)* Not one word! Which has been reimagined with a lively Southwestern flair. *(Continuing to the group.)* Comprised of freshly blessed lamb....

(She reaches for a plate and starts to serve the lamb.)

LYDIA. Lamb?

SUZIE. *(Quick, overriding her, serving another dish.)* Treated with a glaze made from vedalia onions, garlic, cane sugar, ancho chile powder, dried apricots and the blackest of black pepper. Oh my, oh my. Roasted and served with coush coush, that's it's correct pronunciation, "coush coush," tossed with tender root vegetables.

JEFF. What's that stuff on the side?

SUZIE. A kind of charred corn salsa, which I use as kind of, well, relish, which means you can skip it, if you like. My grandmother suffered from colitis so corn is always optional with me.

LYDIA. What is colitis?

SUZIE. I'll explain it later. It's not exactly dinner table conversation.

KHALID. My mother had colitis. It was excruciating for her, so very painful. And she loved food so much, she could deny herself nothing, the nuts and the strawberries, she finally died from it.
SUZIE. I'm so sorry.
LYDIA. But what is it?
JULIA. Excuse me. Where is the rest room?

(SUZIE points her to the pit. She goes.)

ROGER. The lining of the bowels have holes in them, so food gets stuck down there, infected, causes terrible intestinal distress. *(Offers food to seatmate.)* Careful, it's hot.
TERENCE. No, that's not colitis. That's diverticultis. Colitis is—
LYDIA. *(Appalled now.)* Oh no, oh, god, please! I'm so sorry I asked.

(In the corner, JULIA opens a hatch. A huge waft of smoke, red light, appear.)

JULIA. Oh my. Oh my. Is this right?
SUZIE. Yes, yes, go on, it's down the steps and around the corner, a sharp left, you'll see! Who needs wine?

(Perplexed, JULIA goes. The conversation continues. SUZIE serves wine.)

TERENCE. I'm speaking there.
LYDIA. Where?
TERENCE. The Colitis Foundation of America has asked me to speak. Muhammad Ali was there last year.
SUZIE. A Muslim.
LYDIA. He had colitis?
TERENCE. An American Muslim with colitis, yes.

LYDIA. Why did they ask you?
TERENCE. You know, it's a foundation, darling. They need people of a certain stature, I suppose.
LYDIA. Stature, you have stature?
TERENCE. Well ... a little stature goes along way these days. Cheers!

(He drinks.)

SUZIE. Don't be ridiculous, you're very famous. He's famous, just like the rest of you.
LYDIA. I make no claim to be famous.
SUZIE. Well, I'm famous.
JEFF. I'm not famous.
SUZIE. You are now!
TERENCE. I was famous once. Fifteen minutes, or perhaps it was a little less than that.
ROGER. I'm famous. I'm the most famous person here.
SUZIE. Has anyone read Roger's latest novel? He writes one a year. They make big movies out of them. Blockbusters! President Reagan once said Roger was his favorite novelist.
ROGER. Now he doesn't know who the fuck I am. But I still get invitations to things.
LYDIA. And who are you?
KHALID. I'm mere. I'm just a man. A simple man with a simple cause.
SUZIE. Khalid is a scholar and an esteemed specialist in Middle Eastern studies.
ROGER. So?
TERENCE. Well, more wine, anyone? *(Stopping, stunned.)* Good Lord, Suz, this is a terrific bottle. *(Kissing the bottle.)* I'm undone!
SUZIE. How's the lamb everyone?

(Everyone applauds the lamb.)

LYDIA. *(Concerned and hungry.)* Isn't there any uh, salad or anything?
SUZIE. Not until after the main course. Have some of this.

(She offers her the water pitcher. The trap opens and JULIA reappears. She approaches the table, takes her seat.)

JULIA. I found it. My god, It's kind of remarkable really—
SUZIE. It's an experience, isn't it?
JULIA. Well, first of all, it's very, how shall I put it ... Big. And my god! All those endless mirrored walls and ceilings and then on the floor, what was that?
SUZIE. Burnished Venetian amber.
JULIA. Which is all back-lit, you know, so everything just sort of glows.
LYDIA. This sounds incredible.
JULIA. *(Charged, a little angry.)* Girl, you have to see it! I mean, it's big!
SUZIE. It's very special, if I say so myself!
JULIA. There I was, all by myself, you know, and I suddenly became aware of this kind of infinite chorus line reflection of me in every single mirror! I mean, I was just surrounded by ME, hundreds of "ME's" just sitting there you know. And, well, I started to feel sorry, so sorry, like I wanted to apologize but I didn't know to whom. *(Suddenly.)* I mean, it's really less of a bathroom and more of a shrine to our own shit, isn't it?
TERENCE. Wowwee!
SUZIE. No no, it's fine, she's overwhelmed. Is that it, you're overwhelmed by the bathroom?
JULIA. Yes, that's exactly—could I have some of that? *(Recklessly pouring herself wine as she talks.)* I was down there and I thought of my mother and the little excursions we'd take to Bloomingdales. We'd go up to the eighth floor where there were these little mock rooms, all decorated to the hilt, and she'd oohh and ahhh. I

mean this was way better than a trip to the museum for her, it was more like an archeological foray into white people's lives, only you didn't have to make small talk and pretend you were cozy. See, she wished that all that luxury could be mine one day, 'cause that was a sign of real achievement to her. But for me, hanging out in that ballroom you call a bathroom, well, it just made me feel so far away from her and so far away from anything real—look, no offense, Suzie, but don't you think having a gloriously appointed bathroom is the strangest barometer of fulfillment you could ever imagine?

(Cell phone rings. Everyone panics, wondering if it's theirs. It's Roger's.)

SUZIE. Cell phones *verbotten*!

(Some people turn theirs off.)

ROGER. Sorry. It'll only be a moment....

(He steps downstage to talk.)

JULIA. *(Still angry.)* I'm upset. Sorry. I'm just upset. And now you're all staring at me and suddenly, I feel like the only black person in the room.
JEFF. You are the only black person in the room.
SUZIE. I invited Denzel but he cancelled at the last minute. ROG!!!
ROGER. It's my mother!
KHALID. *(To JULIA.)* I'm golden. But in the sun I turn black too.
SUZIE. I'm sorry my bathroom upset you so much. That decorator told me the floor thing would be soothing.
JULIA. *(The truth.)* Forget it. I'm sorry. I just feel so alone, sometimes, in situations like this.

SUZIE. What would make you feel better? Would you like to sing?

JULIA. Oh—no!

SUZIE. A little gospel tune or something? A Whitney Huston song, I love her, although really, she should eat.

JULIA. I'm really not much of a singer.

SUZIE. I'm sure you're wonderful!

JULIA. No, I'm not!! *(Ironic.)* I'm the only black person on earth who can't sing.

SUZIE. *(Not getting it.)* I'm sure that's not true!!

KHALID. I love music. You don't like to sing?

JULIA. Well, actually, I do, I've always loved it. I'm just, really, I'm not very good at it.

SUZIE. Who told you that?

JULIA. Mrs. Gambi, who led the choir in grade school. My cousin Frank. Three separate boyfriends in college.

SUZIE. Well, you can't let them silence you! No no no, listen: If I listened to everyone who told me I was a dingaling, I would never have all this!

ROGER. She's right about that. Nobody believed in her. Except for me, I saw the genius before anybody.

SUZIE. He was heroic. *(To ROGER, back story.)* You were.

TERENCE. Oh god!

SUZIE. *(To TERENCE.)* He was!

JULIA. I think that's different.

LYDIA. No it's not.

KHALID. Why would that be different?

JULIA. Well, because because … you want me to sing?

(Everyone agrees they do.)

SUZIE. Don't you want to?

(JULIA thinks about this. The idea has an odd, friendly appeal to

her.)

JULIA. Actually, I think it would make me feel better.
SUZIE. Well, then you must! Give her room, give her room—

(They encourage her, applauding. She stands to sing, and then starts into a gospel tune or a famous song by a popular black singer. Her voice is spectacularly bad, but she delivers every note with real heartfelt passion. She doesn't necessarily know all the words. Then, after several verses and a chorus, she stops.
She is truly a terrible singer. The group is silenced for a moment, by how awful she is.)

ROGER. That was terrific.

(The group all struggles valiantly to enthusiastically agree.)

TERENCE. Really, just splendid. Who was that who told you you couldn't sing? Complete nonsense.
JULIA. Thank you. You're right, Suzie, I feel a lot better.
KHALID. *(Pouring wine.)* Yes, wonderful, wonderful. I was transfixed.
JULIA. I'm sure.
KHALID. *(Reassuring her.)* You are exquisite. Have some lamb, you must be hungry, and our hostess has outdone herself.
SUZIE. Thank you, sweetheart.
JEFF. And that coush coush stuff, unbelievable. *(To LYDIA.)* Can you have that?
LYDIA. I could if it weren't drenched in lamb fat.
JEFF. Well, it's real good.
TERENCE. I would like to pose a question, and god knows I don't mean to rile or provoke, but why peace? I mean, indeed. Why?
LYDIA. "Why peace?"
TERENCE. Historically it is an anomaly. I think we need to ex-

amine the possibility that peace is not a beneficial or desirable condition for the human race. If it were, it would have been more readily embraced by now.
    JULIA. I disagree.
    TERENCE. Hear me out.
    KHALID. Oh dear. Is this a fly in my glass?
    SUZIE. *(Gasping.)* Oh no! Oh no no, oh no—

(She grabs the glass and takes it off.)

    LYDIA. So peace is still a sort of ...
    KHALID. Chimera....
    LYDIA. A chimera, yes, is that what you mean?

(SUZIE returns, giving KHALID a new wine glass.)

    TERENCE. More along the lines of a child's fairy tale. Happily ever after, the imagined state of bliss which can never be fully or even partially described within the story itself because it is in fact a fantasy.
    LYDIA. So, the human race, people, women, when we say we want peace we don't really mean it.
    TERENCE. Perhaps peace is a romantic assumption that has no grounding in a post-modern utopia.
    LYDIA. Hey. Enough with the British superiority! Everything is so articulate and calming and dismissive when the fact is, this is just another version of some imperialistic old world excuse to be the right one in the room.
    TERENCE. Well. *En garde.*
    LYDIA. *(Riled and direct.)* We don't want peace? Let me tell you something. Women and children want peace and this is, you know, male narcissism, this global male narcissism, that we are all like you, want what you want, greed, winning, well, that's not what's driving the rest of us and the fact is some of us really do want the world to survive. What men want is not what everyone wants!

SUZIE. I'm an incest survivor, too.

LYDIA. No no. Don't do that. We're not victims together here, I'm not a victim and I have no interest in participating in some ludicrous victim identity. Everyone else seems to be really interested in that and I'll tell you something: I am not.

KHALID. Who are you in community with? You must be very lonely.

LYDIA. Because I don't identify myself as a victim, I'm lonely?

SUZIE. I'm never lonely.

KHALID. I'm lonely all the time. Which is why, you see, without community we have no container for our lives.

ROGER. Oh for god's sake. I'm not in community with you. I agree with her.

LYDIA. Don't agree with me. I am so not in community with you.

JEFF. God, this is good.

SUZIE. Thank you. I had help! *(LYDIA, mocking her.)* Thousands of slaves!

TERENCE. Stunning. Bravo!

SUZIE. And wait till you see what else is coming!

TERENCE. Don't tell!

SUZIE. I won't! I won't!

JEFF. Are you going to have any?

LYDIA. No, you can have it all.

JEFF. You could have the corn stuff.

SUZIE. It's relish, dear. Relish

LYDIA. What's in it?

SUZIE. Fresh September corn off the cob, red pepper, onion and roasted red peppers.

LYDIA. Fine. I'll take it.

(She takes the bowl.)

KHALID. Couldn't I have a drop of something, something hard, such as whiskey or scotch ....

SUZIE. *(On her way to the trap door.)* Say no more! Scotch with the meal, *muy macho*.

(She disappears.)

KHALID. I need a little hard stuff on occasion. Helps me to forget.

TERENCE. *(Toasting.)* Here's to forgetting.

LYDIA. Forgetting what?

KHALID. Oh, you know. Pain. Loss. Death.

ROGER. Whoa!

TERENCE. Bravo! It isn't a dinner party until someone mentions the Grim Reaper, that's when you know you've really hit your stride.

KHALID. But death, that is not a metaphor! There is real danger here! You are being cast as enemies of god! If this is the perception, the call to fatwa is holy!

TERENCE. All right then, let me just say it: I detest all Abrahmic religions. Everyone killing in the name of God, please.

ROGER. I'm not killing anybody in the name of God. I'm just defending myself.

JULIA. Yes, but it's logic like that which has us talking about nuclear war again. Could you pass the relish?

LYDIA. Okay, but I need it back!

ROGER. What are we supposed to do, just sit there?

TERENCE. Wait wait wait. I want some of that.

(He intercepts the relish.)

JULIA. That's what Ghandi did. That and organized peaceful protest.

LYDIA. You don't want that, it's not that good.

ROGER. As part of a strategy.

JULIA. *(Angry now.)* As part of true belief! Come on! If you guys are saying "nuclear war" and Ghandi is saying "peaceful protest," well, I'm going to go stand over here, with Ghandi! *(Furious.)* Give me the relish!

TERENCE. All right, all right!

JULIA. Sorry. It's just, there comes a point when peace isn't some crazy ideal, it's just common fucking sense!

LYDIA. Can I have that back? It's the only thing without a face.

ROGER. You can't just ask for peace! It's too simple!

JULIA. Why?

JEFF. I'd like some of that, too.

LYDIA. Too late!

ROGER. You can't just talk about a paradigm for peace with people as nuts as Hitler!

JULIA. Oh, and we're not nuts? We're enslaved to oil, we're poisoning the planet, and we're ready to kill our own children, send them into battle, to preserve our right to do that!

ROGER. That's simplistic.

JULIA. No it's not! It's fucking not!

SUZIE. *(Re-emerging.) Est voila.* Bourbon! Pour Monsuier Khalid.

TERENCE. Our buds of taste are all a flutter, dear Suzie. You missed death, global annihilation—

JULIA. Ghandi.

TERENCE. And Hitler.

LYDIA. *(Pointing to ROGER.)* He brought him up, not me.

SUZIE. Good. Oh, good!

TERENCE. I can't remember the last time something tasted so good. I did have a marvelous white rat at the Royal Palace in Constantinople.

ROGER. I ate there once. Chocolate fucking bugs and shit.

(He pulls out a pack of cigarettes.)

LYDIA. *(Reacting.)* Hey, hey, hey!!!
ROGER. Oh, here it comes—

TERENCE. Tremendous! Smoking at the dinner table, we'll have our own little world war three.

(He pulls out his own pack.)

LYDIA. I'm not kidding about this. This is not good!
ROGER. Look. I don't care! I grew up in a different time.
SUZIE. We all did, dear Roger. Terence!
ROGER. It was considered civilized!
LYDIA. So was the atom bomb!
ROGER. The atom bomb ended the war! Truman was our greatest president!
LYDIA. He dropped the bomb!
SUZIE. *(Springing up.)* But the problem is, you can't smoke in here because it will destabilize the air quality. Because of that nasty eternal fire, I have to have my air flown in. Now, come on, Roggie, you can smoke down here.
ROGER. *(As they go.)* I just thought this would be a little more relaxing, honey. You know. Sinatra. A band.
SUZIE. Just wait until you see what's coming later!
ROGER. Is it a band?

(They exit through the trap. LYDIA watches, while the others eat.)

LYDIA. Wait a minute. So it's burning, but the air is pure? Is anyone else having trouble with this?
KHALID. Paradox. Like America itself. Which is at once both the thing and its opposite.
TERENCE. Hats off to paradox.

(He lights up.)

KHALID. "*Aureo Apprehensio.*"

JULIA. Golden Understanding.

TERENCE. Enlightenment.

JULIA. Faith.

TERENCE. Faith, oh no no, please, God. Faith. What the devil is it, faith?

JEFF. It's just—faith.

KHALID. Faith replaces the cynical ambivalence we all feel as a defense to the world.

TERENCE. You haven't a clue then.

JULIA. Yes I do. The universe makes perfect sense, just not to us.

TERENCE. Oh good. That clears it up then, clears it right up.

JULIA. Faith gives us the stamina to accomplish the difficult task of being human. *(SUZIE and ROGER emerge again.)* You know, the Bible says—

TERENCE. Oh, god. The Bible. Here it comes, here it comes, a gentle segue into biblical topics leading straight into the Promised Land and the Chosen People!

ROGER. *(Beginning to exit again.)* You should have let me finish that cigarette.

TERENCE. Bloody Israel!

SUZIE. No, no, no you can't keep leaving!

ROGER. Don't start in on Israel!

TERENCE. My mother is Jewish. I can say whatever I want.

JEFF. Is there any salad?

SUZIE. Yes dear, you're so right.

LYDIA. Oh good, oh good.

SUZIE. Terence!

(She gestures to his cigarette, which he puts out. Another table appears in the doorway. This one sports salad.)

ROGER. Look here, Israel is America's moral and philosophical partner, and its founders were people like us, fleeing oppression, and their democracy is the only one in the region, based on freedom and tolerance.

KHALID. Tolerance?

TERENCE. Yes, yes, I've heard all about it. My mother wanted to go to Palestine, a.k.a. "Israel," very badly at one point.

ROGER. Good for her.

TERENCE. Well I told her, "Mum, dear, it's a bad bloody idea. A overzealous, messianic shithole of an idea, oh, and by the way, what do you suppose we're going to do with all those Arabs after we take their land away from them?

ROGER. Take it away? Israel was deemed a sovereign state by the United Nations in 1948.

TERENCE. Take it away and give it to a whole bunch of sophisticated Jews so that they can suddenly turn themselves into peasant farmers, what kind of an idea is this?

ROGER. They turned a desert into a garden for crying out loud.

TERENCE. They stole the fucking water! Besides which, the occupation—

ROGER. Here we go—

TERENCE. And I don't give a shit! That is precisely what it is—

ROGER. It's their Goddamn Biblical Homeland!!

TERENCE. Not the State, the occupation, presents a guaranteed injustice—

ROGER. Golan Heights, the Sinai Peninsula, the West Bank were all gained after Israel was attacked in a war!!!

TERENCE. May I finish!! Injustice against the Arabs—

ROGER. They didn't even want that land—

TERENCE. Let me finish. And now, to add insult to injustice, this fence—this wall—

ROGER. Mark Twain went there at the end of the nineteenth— The Balfour Declaration! Ah, you don't know your history! There were Jews already there! But as soon as they claimed it as their homeland, every Arab in the world bragged—bragged!—that they would drive them into the sea!

TERENCE. Four decades of Arabs suffering under the most humiliating and degraded conditions—

ROGER. Humiliated by fellow Arabs who never lift a finger to help their own—

TERENCE. Children murdered in the streets by Israeli soldiers—

ROGER. Palestinian maniacs blowing themselves up—

TERENCE. Nobody's hands are clean over there! Nobody's hands are clean! And now, the world's finally recognizing the disastrous error behind the whole bloody thing! And as far as I'm concerned anyone who doesn't agree with me is a fucking idiot!

ROGER. There's no need to lose your temper.

TERENCE. Look here, the point is, if Jews born in Yonkers, or Los Angeles or Cleveland for god sakes, have a right to a blasted bloody state in Palestine, then it should follow Palestinians born in Jerusalem also have a right to a state in Palestine, or how about some carved up Palestinian settlements smack in the middle of West Palm Beach or East Hampton for that matter!! *(To KHALID.)* Any time you want to leap in, be my guest.

KHALID. No, you're doing just fine.

ROGER. The world will always use a double standard toward the Jews because because they hate Jews.

SUZIE. Wonderful! What a wonderful point! I'd like to turn your attention, if I may, to the salad!

ROGER. This is the prelude to another holocaust.

TERENCE. Oh the big "H." I knew you were going to say that!

ROGER. Arabs want a final solution, not just to Israel. But to Jews! All Jews, everywhere!! *(Pointedly.)* And that means you!!

KHALID. Stop. Stop, please. Your position is so cruel and demeaning to all of us. To my people, to your people.

ROGER. Your leaders supported Sadaam Hussein.

KHALID. So did yours!

ROGER. They supported Bin Laden.

KHALID. So did yours!

ROGER. At the moment when Israel was ready to make peace,

they declared war.

KHALID. A Jewish extremist murdered his own peacemaker! You see, tragic mistakes have been made by both sides, but we must not despair. Please.

SUZIE. Such a lively debate. Wonderful, really, bravo to everyone. Now, for the salad. I, for one have never been a fan of frisee. It's too wild on the plate. I do a nice mélange of microgreens and baby arugula dotted with pomegranate seeds in a spicy orange vinagrette, tossed with whole toasted walnuts.

LYDIA. Walnuts!! I'm fucking allergic to walnuts. I'm sorry, I'm sorry, I'm so so hungry. And aside from the relish and that thingiedo which was the size of a pea, I can't eat anything.

SUZIE. *(Annoyed.)* Well, you could just pick the walnuts out dear, if you must. Julia could I impose on you?

JULIA. Of course.

SUZIE. You really are the perfect dinner guest.

(They clear the table. She starts to serve.)

JEFF. Uh, sorry, where's the dressing?

SUZIE. It's totally dressed! And everything picked fresh from my own little hydroponic greenhouse.

ROGER. She does it all. She's a goddamn renaissance mogul.

SUZIE. You have such a way with words.

JULIA. I love to garden.

SUZIE. I'm just about to launch a great gardening website.

TERENCE. *(Pouring.) Vino vite in vitro wino—*

KHALID. Slow down, man.

SUZIE. You can literally create a garden of your own design, whatever you fancy—

TERENCE. No no, what is it, in *vino vino*?

KHALID. *In vino veritas.* Give me some of that.

SUZIE. Formal English—

TERENCE. In weeno-weri-what?

SUZIE. Rustic Americana—
KHALID. Yes, that's it—
SUZIE. Or even a sort of pan Japanese reflecting pool and surrounding serenity garden. And all virtual!

(TERENCE toasts KHALID, laughing.)

TERENCE. *(Grandly.)* Here's to the last days of the Roman Empire!
SUZIE. We're specifically targeting people with allergies.
JEFF. What's in this dressing? It's really good.
SUZIE. Oh it's so easy. But it's secret. I have to have some secrets, don't I?
JULIA. Virtual gardens. That's depressing. We're all becoming part of an electronic herd of lemmings and rhinoceri.
LYDIA. Rhinoceri? Is that really the plural?
TERENCE. Of course it is.
LYDIA. Oh, you think you know everything.
SUZIE. The British really are better educated than we are, dear. There's no use being defensive about it. Have you ever seen the British version of *The Weakest Link*? It's much harder than the American version.
LYDIA. American television. Ick. No wonder the rest of the world hates us.
KHALID. Yes, yes! You all berate the Arab culture for its impulse to, to to—
TERENCE. Theocratic dictatorship?
KHALID. "Theocratic dictatorship," yes, thank you—
TERENCE. Thank Cambridge.
KHALID. —but you, at the same time you overwhelm the world with cultural dictatorship.
LYDIA. *The Weakest Link* is not culture. God help us. Is that culture?
JEFF. I've never actually seen it.

JULIA. What we have to do is figure out how to support artists. Everywhere.
TERENCE. Oh for god's sake.
ROGER. Funding the arts!
TERENCE. Funding the arts!
ROGER. Grow up!

(They find this hysterical.)

JULIA. Why? Musicians, poets, painters—I need more dressing—
SUZIE. No. No. Try it again!
JULIA. It's the definition of culture, people finding their reflection in art—I really do think, Suzie—
SUZIE. It's swimming, already! I won't let you drown it!
JEFF. Art?
SUZIE. I love poetry!
ROGER. But no one's going to fund it! Please!
SUZIE. "You are the weakest link. Good bye."

(They laugh at each other.)

JULIA. But the way things are going now, pretty soon the only culture left will be in Disney pavilions, or on bad TV.
SUZIE. I love CNN. I couldn't live without it. Reading puts me to sleep.
LYDIA. You just said you loved poetry, how can you love poetry if you don't read?
SUZIE. You're so contentious! Why are you attacking me all the time?
LYDIA. I'm not attacking, I'm asking a question.
SUZIE. Would anyone like more salad?
JULIA. I'd like more dressing.
SUZIE. All right, all right! I surrender under protest!

(She goes for the salad dressing.)

    JEFF. Oh, great, can I have some too?
    SUZIE. *(Outraged.)* Oh!
    ROGER. Okay, I'm not going to say culture is superfluous, because that's what you all expect me to say. But, it's kind of superfluous, especially now.
    LYDIA. What are you talking about! You write novels!
    ROGER. And I make a damn good living at it, too. 'Cause there's a market for what I write about!
    SUZIE. Who's seen *Mamma Mia*? I can get you tickets.
    KHALID. Is this spearmint? I'm tasting spearmint.
    SUZIE. Thank you for noticing! You subtle, brilliant man.
    LYDIA. I think Julia's right. We have to nurture culture as a living reality. It can't just be survival of the richest.
    TERENCE. Or the best reviewed.
    LYDIA. Oh, not critics. Let's not go there—
    JULIA. Well, I have to confess, I'm far more afraid of *The Times Book Review* than I am of Islamic terrorists. They massacred my last book. It took me five years to write that.
    SUZIE. What was it about?
    JULIA. It was called *Engaging the Moral Eye*. It was basically a series of talks and essays about creativity and community.

(Roger burps loudly.)

    SUZIE. Roger! Oh, please!
    JULIA. The reviewer was really cruel.
    TERENCE. Happened to me, once. I was on Zoloft for a year. Now I think I have it in perspective.

(He drinks a big slug of wine.)

SUZIE. They usually like my books. You just have to know what they like. They don't want to be touched. They want to be entertained.

JULIA. *(To SUZIE.)* You're right. This critic didn't want to be touched. He just didn't want to be touched.

TERENCE. Well, have you seen the people they employ over there? Who would want to touch them?

(They all laugh.)

JULIA. Yes, I have to say when I heard someone had sent Anthrax to *The Times*, my first thought was, "Isn't that toooo bad."

(They all roar with laughter, except ROGER.)

ROGER. Sour grapes, sour fucking grapes!

SUZIE. Roger! Language! You know how I feel about that "fucking" word!

ROGER. She uses it! And she wants to bomb *The New York Times*, for Christ's sake!

JULIA. I'm kidding!

ROGER. *(Takes SUZIE in.)* You know, Suzie, when you get stern like that I find you damn attractive.

SUZIE. Really?

TERENCE. What one has to wonder regarding *The Times* is simply, is it the paper of record, or the pacifier of the bourgeoisie? The latter has an equally good ring to it, with the added advantage of being true.

KHALID. Not the bourgeoisie, no no. The rich. The pacifier of the rich.

ROGER. How is money the issue? How did we get here again?

KHALID. You have too much!

TERENCE. Oh it's not just *The Times*. Print news is over. All five sources of television news are now divisions of large conglomerates.

JULIA. Pass the wine, please.

TERENCE. AOL Time Warner, General Electric, VIACOM, Rupert Murdoch, and, lest we forget, Disney!

SUZIE. Mickey Mouse?

TERENCE. Yes, Mickey Mouse controls your news, Suzie. The conglomerate vision of America is replacing the democratic ideal and what's emerging is an empire devoted to the bad thinking of a self-protecting elite class. And you know what happens to empires, don't you?

(As he hands the wine to JULIA, he spills it all over her. People stand and scatter.)

JULIA. *(Overlap.)* Oh, I'm sorry, I'm so sorry—
SUZIE. Oh dear, oh dear.
KHALID. Quite all right—
JULIA. Here—
SUZIE. We'll just put this over it.
JULIA. I'm sorry.
SUZIE. Don't worry.
TERENCE. The first wine has been spilt! Which clearly means—we need another bottle!

(SUZIE goes to the sideboard.)

SUZIE. You're drinking too fast!
TERENCE. No dinner party is any good unless someone is drinking too fast. *(As he kisses her.)* I'm doing it for you, darling.
KHALID. *(To JULIA.)* I like your stockings. They're very smooth.
JULIA. You've had too much to drink, Khalid. I'm not wearing stockings.
KHALID. Oh.

SUZIE. Whooo! We're not supposed to be getting intimate, you two!!
TERENCE. *(A drunken non sequitur.)* But we haven't really looked at globalization yet.

(People moan in protest.)

ROGER. I am so sick of that word!
JEFF. I can never figure out what it's supposed to mean.
KHALID. It is at the root of everything—everything—
JEFF. Yeah, but what does it mean?
SUZIE. Oh, dear don't salt that, no no—
TERENCE. How to explain "globalization."
LYDIA. Here we go. He's revving up—
TERENCE. As the world continues to experience the destructive power of the global marketplace, the backlash has produced a whole set of ideologies—communism, socialism, fascism--all of which originally promised to take the sting out of capitalism. Now that these ideologies have been discredited there's nothing that can truly soften the cruelty of capitalism and still produce rising standards of living for the working poor. The only thing left standing is modern fundamentalism, which is why we are where we are.

(A beat.)

JEFF. I followed that.
SUZIE. I did too.
JEFF. Is he getting clearer because we're getting drunker?
SUZIE. Is drunker a word?
KHALID. So what we have is the very rich—
SUZIE. And, the very drunk—

(She laughs, so does JEFF.)

TERENCE. And underneath them, grabbers, criminals, thieves.
LYDIA. You know who predicted this? Marx.
TERENCE. No! God! Don't say Marx!
KHALID. This is true!
TERENCE. I didn't say Marx!
KHALID. Those who can't make the transition to the fast world will create their own counterculture. Which will by necessity be defined as criminal by the ruling money elite.
ROGER. History is turning over. That's what we're looking at here. The last time history turned over, in Europe, the death of monarchy, you know what the consequences were? Two hundred years of war, culminating in the Holocaust, Stalin and the death camps. Eight million dead in Europe, twenty-two million in Russia. That's the possibility we're facing. And you can't dismiss me because I believe in going to war to save ourselves!
KHALID. Oh dear.

(He drinks.)

JULIA. No one's dismissing you. Hardly.
ROGER. *(Off LYDIA.)* She is.
LYDIA. I'm not!
ROGER. You're rolling your eyes, I see you.
LYDIA. Well, now I am.
ROGER. Is there any Ranch?
SUZIE. Ranch!?! Oh no, Roger. Please. This is the worse than the profanity.
TERENCE. Or Marx!
SUZIE. I think people are evolving, but the power system isn't.

(A beat.)

KHALID. What?

JULIA. What?
TERENCE. What?
SUZIE. Yes. All those guys, the ones on the top are just spinning, see, but a lot of other people aren't. We're ready for a new approach, but they can't relate because they're just stuck.

(Another beat.)

JULIA. We're evolving but the power system isn't. That's very good, Suzie.
SUZIE. Merci.
LYDIA. Rampant capitalism obviously brings problems everywhere, let's face it, it doesn't serve America, either, we're just drowning in greed and our culture is collapsing—but isn't something else going on in much of the Muslim world? It suppresses, hides and destroys the feminine. The degree to which men try to hurt and annihilate women is the degree to which they have driven themselves insane.
KHALID. Yes, yes, this is very profound, what she is saying.
ROGER. Oh brother.
LYDIA. Oh brother what?
ROGER. Oh brother, I'd like more salad.
LYDIA. *(Curt.)* I realize that because America is still deep in its own misogyny some people will not be able to understand this.
ROGER. I just think that when you reduce something to your own little personal agenda, you're not being very useful.
LYDIA. I'm not taking this on.
ROGER. Take this on. It's their culture. Their culture, and you're trying to impose your idea of culture on everyone.
LYDIA. No, I'm not!
ROGER. You're as big an imperialist capitalist whatever as me or him or any globalization nightmare junkie you're so ready to condemn. You want the whole world to look just the way you like it for

you and your little proto-feminist lesbian friends.
TERENCE. And they're off!
SUZIE. No, I worry about that too. Maybe we've just interfered too much already. I see all those men in their robes and their turbans and it's like looking at people living in a different country.
KHALID. Actually, it is still a medieval culture, many Arabs take great pride in that, and feel powerfully that their identity must be protected.
SUZIE. And then all those guns! We gave them all those guns! I saw it on television last week and thought, hasn't anyone ever watched Star Trek?

(There is a short, surprised moment.)

TERENCE. What a leap! Spectacular! A veritable triple lutz of a conversational segue!
SUZIE. Thank you, darling. Because the prime directive is you mustn't interfere in more primitive cultures. You just don't go onto someone else's planet and mess around with what they're doing there.
LYDIA. Yes, but then Captain Kirk would just sleep with all the women.
TERENCE. I actually enjoyed that aspect of the original series. The later ones did away with all the sex, it just wasn't as good.
JEFF. You know what that reminds me of? I thought about? That Star Trek episode where there were those two guys who were trying to kill each other, and they looked exactly alike, they had faces that were half black and half white. Everyone on the Enterprise thought they were identical twins or something, but then it turned out that they were really mirror images of each other. One guy was black on the left side of his face, and the other guy was black on the right side of his face. And their whole planet had destroyed itself because of that difference that seemed so big to them, but nobody else could even see it, really. And then at the end of the episode, they killed each

other.

(A moment of silence.)

ROGER. That was a good episode.
TERENCE. That's touching, really it is. But, honestly, isn't it just one step away from, "Can't we all just get along?" I regret being the one to once again assume the mantle of reality—
ROGER. Ah Christ.
TERENCE. But the fact is that we've never gotten along! Human history is a blood bath. *(Emphatically.)* Killing each other is what we do!

(LYDIA stands.)

LYDIA. I'm sorry. I've having a little trouble breathing all of a sudden.
SUZIE. I told you to take the walnuts out!
LYDIA. It's not the walnuts. I'm—the fact is, I have to, well, actually—I'm pregnant. And, the fact is, thinking about bringing a child into this—*(Increasingly upset.)* Bringing a child into all of this—terror, and and—I have to go, I have to go for a moment—

(She goes to the back of the room, opens the trap. The smoke comes up. She descends.)

SUZIE. Oh, my. I didn't know. She's pregnant. And I didn't make anything that she could eat. I feel terrible! No, you can't have anymore of the salad, Roger—you can eat the meat, but the rest of the salad is for Lydia. Here, somebody pick the walnuts out.

(She hands ROGER's salad to JEFF.)

JULIA. Maybe she could use a few crackers!

SUZIE. Crackers? Yes, crackers! Of course. That's an excellent idea. I'll be right back. *(She goes, opens the trap. The smoke comes out. She looks back at them before disappearing.)* "Saltines" will be just the thing.

(She goes into the smoke. JEFF picks out the walnuts.)

ROGER. Okay. I don't want anybody expecting me to be nicer because she's pregnant. I hate that.

(The trap opens. LYDIA comes out, followed by SUZIE. She carries a box of saltines.)

SUZIE. Everything's fine! She's had a little throw up, and feels much better.
JULIA. Here here, maybe you should have some water?
LYDIA. Yes, thank you.
SUZIE. We saved the salad, I'm so sorry that I didn't—I just didn't realize—oh and even the sight of all this meat and all that salmon!
LYDIA. No no, I'm fine—these saltines are a big help—

(She eats them hungrily.)

KHALID. How far along are you?
LYDIA. Uh, three months.
ROGER. *(Dry.)* Who's the lucky guy?
LYDIA. I, um—I don't know, actually.
SUZIE. Oh, how refreshing! And we can just talk about it now, at the dinner table. When I was young, this would not have been possible. Was it a petri dish sort of thing, all anonymous? So many lesbians are having babies this way now, and it's so funny, because you know, it means that we really don't need men anymore! We can just go

ahead and have babies without them!

LYDIA. It wasn't that.

ROGER. But you don't know who the father is? How'd that happen?

LYDIA. Okay, it's not a petri dish sort of thing but it's also not an I'm a slut sort of thing. It's more like a sleazy, I can't believe I got myself into the biggest mess imaginable sort of thing. You don't want to hear it.

(All voraciously agree that they should hear it.)

ALL. Oh yes we do!
TERENCE. Absolutely.
JULIA. I want to hear it.
LYDIA. Okay. There was this guy I was involved with in college. And he was, it was one of those relationships that are completely maddening and inexplicable but passionate and deeply truthful, we were—but we were also you know, twenty, twenty one, and he was completely insane.

TERENCE. Thus, your dynamic attraction to him.

LYDIA. I swear to god, talking to this guy was like diving to the bottom of a lake. And sex was unbelievable.

SUZIE. I like this story already.

LYDIA. He was also a cheater, cheating on me, and then lying about it—

SUZIE. Good sex and cheating. I love this dinner party!

LYDIA. —and I would find out and try to get out of the relationship, and he would become desperate, but not desperate enough to actually stop sleeping with other women—

SUZIE. Of course not.
TERENCE. And the sex?
LYDIA. Unbelievable!
KHALID. What did you do?

LYDIA. I finally, I tried honestly for over a year to get myself out of this thing, but he would, and then I would—oh god. I do think he loved me, I know he did—

TERENCE. In that particular way that cheaters love.

LYDIA. Yes, yes, so one day I finally said to him, I never want to see you again. I don't want you to ever speak my name again. You are not allowed to even think about me. We do not inhabit the same planet. Stay away from me forever.

JULIA. Good for you!

SUZIE. Then what happened?

LYDIA. That fucking internet. He did a search. I shouldn't have written back! But it was twenty years ago!

ROGER. Cut to the chase. You got back together—

SUZIE. She's doing it, she's telling the story, don't rush her, Roger!

LYDIA. I'm involved with someone! I've been in a wonderful relationship for five years! I love this man deeply.

TERENCE. But the sex, with the other guy—

KHALID. I want to hear about the man she's with.

JEFF. Yeah.

SUZIE. No, no, we want to hear about the sexy guy from her past—

JULIA and SUZIE. *(Chiming in.)* The sexy guy, the sexy guy!

LYDIA. He lives in London now. I had a conference, just a three day thing—

ROGER. A conference?

SUZIE. ROG!!

LYDIA. So I called him, at his work, and an Irishman answered the phone.

JULIA. He's Irish?

LYDIA. He didn't used to be! When I knew him, he was from Illinois! But he's been living in Ireland, apparently, for ten years, and now he has an Irish accent.

SUZIE. I love accents.

LYDIA. And then I said, would you still like to meet for a coffee, and he said we should go to someplace very public. The coffee shop at the Barbicon Center.

TERENCE. Ewwww.

LYDIA. He was very clear about this, in his new Irish accent. So I went out there, and it's this huge concrete—thing—

TERENCE. Yes, it's a monstrosity.

LYDIA. Like a maze—giant buildings with windows—

TERENCE. A complete fiasco.

LYDIA. It took me fifteen minutes to find the coffee shop.

TERENCE. You should try to find the bathroom.

LYDIA. So I'm standing in line, wondering if he's going to actually show up, when I hear someone behind me saying my name in an Irish accent— "Lydya, Lydya."

JEFF. Wow!

JULIA. God!

LYDIA. The first thing I thought was thank god, he looks twenty years older. But then we talked for a while, and—

TERENCE. Yes yes and then—

SUZIE. Let her tell it!

LYDIA. I asked him what he did, and he told me he traveled all over the world, doing some sort of healthcare something—but he couldn't be specific—

TERENCE. Wait wait wait—

SUZIE. Stop interrupting!

TERENCE. Just a minute, darling. Irish? Over-sexed nonspecific world traveler who likes to meet at the Barbicon Center?

LYDIA. Yes.

TERENCE. He's in the I.R.A.!

LYDIA. That's what I thought!

JULIA. Did you really think that?

LYDIA. I wasn't thinking. Which is why I spent most of the

weekend in bed with him.

(The whole group cheers.)

    TERENCE. *(Rising.)* Bravo! Well done! You spitfire! You goddess!
    SUZIE. It's the mystery. That's so hard to resist.
    TERENCE. You slept with a terrorist! I find that fascinating, in light of today's conversation.
    JULIA. He wasn't a terrorist. He just couldn't commit.
    SUZIE. He was a terrorist of the heart!
    LYDIA. I don't know what he was. It was overwhelming, being with him again. But he was never someone you could count on.
    ROGER. To say the least.
    LYDIA. So I went home and thought that was fun, but not a threat, I didn't want it to be a threat to my—the man I'm with, I love him so deeply, and he is someone you can make a life with—and now I'm pregnant and he's so thrilled, just thrilled—and I—
    ROGER. You cheated.
    LYDIA. Yes, I did. I did.
    TERENCE. Cheated, schmeated. She's a goddess! That's what goddesses do!
    JULIA. Don't tell him.
    LYDIA. I shouldn't tell him, should I?
    ROGER. Here we go.
    KHALID. No, she mustn't tell him.
    TERENCE. I think she has to. Loose the shackles! Live free!
    LYDIA. He's so happy.
    JULIA. You can't tell him.
    ROGER. This is why men get pissed off at women, you know. It's got nothing to do with the feminine in the culture blah blah blah—
    KHALID. She cannot tell him! Why tell him, why make him miserable, when they have love?
    SUZIE. I don't know what you should do, dear. Have a cracker.

(She gives her a cracker. She eats.)

ROGER. You know—this story is a bit a surprise. I didn't actually think you liked men.
LYDIA. That's a deep misunderstanding. I want the world to be whole. I want women to be included. That doesn't mean I hate men. "Hating men" is hardly my problem.
JEFF. Don't tell him. *(Beat.)* I agree with that guy. What's the point? Just have your baby and be happy.
SUZIE. There, see! Isn't this nice? We're all agreeing. I knew we could. And as a reward for all of you, being so nice to each other, so nice to dear Lydia—it's time for the surprise!
JULIA. Suzie, please, no more food! You have to just give us few minutes to rest or we'll explode!
TERENCE. Yes, can't eat another bite. Maybe one. And a little more wine. I'm keeping track now.
SUZIE. No no, not food. Tonight's special guest.
TERENCE. Oh, I thought I was the special guest.
ROGER. I thought I was.

(They both laugh.)

SUZIE. Of course you're all special, you know I think that or you wouldn't be here. *(Pleased with herself.)* But in addition to all my favorite people, I did manage to tempt a rather interesting young man to stop by for just a few minutes. To answer some of the many questions we've all been discussing tonight in such a lively fashion. I have a terrorist! *(She throws a chador over her head.)* Mohammed, darling, we're ready for you! Come on in! *(MOHAMMED comes out. JEFF stands, backs away from the table.)* Did you have any trouble parking? Or did one of your friends drive you in his taxi?

(MOHAMMED approaches the table, sullen.)

MOHAMMED. These are the people you spoke of? The ones who are interested in our story? You say you want to know us. Is that what you want?

SUZIE. Yes, darling—

MOHAMMED. The world does not want to know the Arab. You only want to erase the Arab. You want to take our land, and steal our oil, to corrupt our women, demean our culture, and degrade our god. That is what you want.

SUZIE. Oh, now don't be negative! It's a party! This is Julia, and Roger, Lydia, Terence, Jeff, he's a fireman, and Khalid, he's an Arab, like you.

KHALID. *(Speaking first.)* Salam Aleichem.

MOHAMMED. You greet me with the words of our people. But you are no true Arab.

KHALID. I am a true Arab, my friend.

(MOHAMMED immediately starts to insult KHALID. KHALID starts to shout back at him.)

MOHAMMED. Anta mush aarabee, kafir, tarak't allah, tarak't allah wa ah'lak, aarr, anta fadeeheh al aarab, anta as'wa min yahudi— [Translation: You are no Arab, infidel, you have abandoned your god, you have abandoned your god and your people, shame, you are a disgrace to all Arabs!]

KHALID. *(Overlap.)* Mujrim, ma hada ra'yeh lil jan'nah, shou aal'mak min al'lah, tarak't allah, yashtanizz min'nak al'all— [Translation: Murderer! No one is going to paradise for these acts, what do you know of god? Monster! You have abandoned your god! You disgust god!]

TERENCE. Whoa whoa—

ROGER. Back off, asshole—

JEFF. Get him out of here!

SUZIE. Oh, dear—

JULIA. *(Shouting them all down.)* Please! Stop it, please! *(There is a moment of silence.)* Perhaps we should, as Suzie suggests, take the opportunity to, um, try to have a more lively understanding of each other.

ROGER. Has anybody frisked this guy? Check his shoes!

SUZIE. Oh, no, he's promised me not to do anything like that here, haven't you? Everyone sit. And let's get him a seat, there's an extra chair somewhere.... Here, catch up, have some wine.

(She grabs some wine bottles.)

JULIA. Muslims don't drink, Suzie.

SUZIE. But Khalid has been a complete fish, all night!

JULIA. Strict Muslims don't drink. Fundamentalists.

SUZIE. Oh.

ROGER. Not that it stopped them from getting tanked the night before they blew up the World Trade Center.

MOHAMMED. Here is one of your famous American fireman. He is no hero. We are heroes, we do what we do for Allah, we know we are dying. They die without knowing. They are no hero. We die for paradise.

KHALID. No one is going to paradise for these acts!

MOHAMMED. You dine with the infidels!

TERENCE. He dines exquisitely with the infidels.

KHALID. You are the infidel, sir! These people, all of them, are the people of god!

MOHAMMED. You dine with them, you are God's enemy—

KHALID. You murder innocents, women and children—

MOHAMMED. U.S.A., the first terrorist in the history of mankind. You drop an atomic bomb which killed hundreds of thousands of women and children, kill them by burning them to death. You dropped the atomic bomb! Nobody else. In every single war you go to, you kill civilians and innocent people, not soldiers. And you go to wars more than any other country in history. Including the massacre of your own Native Peoples. I'm a terrorist? I only support terrorism so long as it's against the United States government, and against Israel, because you are more than terrorists, you are butchers and liars and hypocrites.

(There is a terrible pause at this. KHALID speaks.)

KHALID. Of all the people killed or harmed in some way by this attack, you cannot name one who was against you or your cause. You didn't care. Just so long as you left dead bodies, and people hurt. You are not fit to represent Islam. Your god is death. You say you act in the name of Allah, but that is a dark lie. You are a barbarian, a scourge, part of a group of rejects of the noble Muslim civilization.

(The terrorist starts to yell at KHALID in Arabic. KHALID yells over him.)

MOHAMMED. Ana baa'raf alle aa'malou wa laysh aa'malou, shou aal'mak min al'lah, kafir, khan't asss'lak, anta fatheehat all aarab— [Translation: I know what I do and why I do it, what do you know of God? Infidel! You betrayed your race! You are a disgrace to all Arabs!]
KHALID. *(Overriding him.)* You adore not Allah but the evil that you yourself have become!

(MOHAMMED jumps on the table, grabbing a dinner fork or breaking a bottle of wine. He is about to attack KHALID. The whole table starts to yell. ROGER and TERENCE and JEFF finally tackle him.)

SUZIE. Oh dear. No, no, no. Please! Mohammed you promised. Don't. Roger!

TERENCE. *(Overlap.)* Good heavens! Everyone stay calm. This situation is under control—
JULIA. *(Overlap.)* Please, stop. Please. Don't hit him, don't hit him!
KHALID. *(Overlap.)* Dear God. This is a nightmare. Please, I beg you, don't harm each other.
LYDIA. *(Overlap.)* Whoa. Somebody call the cops. Suzie call the cops.
SUZIE. *(Overlap.)* Oh, no, no.

(JEFF slugs him, hard. MOHAMMED falls to the floor, still. They all are silenced for a moment.)

TERENCE. Completely under control.
SUZIE. Okay, that was not as much fun as I thought it would be.
LYDIA. Well, what are we going to do with him now? You can't just leave him lie there.
JULIA. He's hurt.
JEFF. Good.
JULIA. Good?
ROGER. Those crazy Muslims.
LYDIA. Not all—
TERENCE. No no, not all Muslims.
JULIA. Not all, don't do that—
ROGER. *(Brushing them off.)* Ahhh! We're going to have to tie him up, Suze!
SUZIE. I have just the thing! Something from nothing, you take the napkin, fold it on the diagonal, a twist and a twirl and there you are. More linens, will that help?

(She grabs a napkin, folds it quickly and ties it to another one, gives it to JEFF, who ties MOHAMMED's hands together and gags him while they continue to debate the situation.)

TERENCE. *(To KHALID.)* Are you all right?
LYDIA. I don't think this is a good idea.
JULIA. What are you doing!?
LYDIA. I don't think this is a good idea.
ROGER. These fundamentalists are crazy.
TERENCE. There are Jewish fundamentalists as well. Who do you think is living in all those settlements?
JULIA. *(Off JEFF.)* That's enough!
ROGER. You're just an anti-Semitic S.O.B, aren't you?
TERENCE. I'm half-Jewish, Fucko!
ROGER. A self-hating half Jewish anti-Semitic S.O.B, then.
JULIA. Please!
TERENCE. Whenever I listen to people like you, I have to confess I feel the freedom of speech is overrated.
JULIA. Please!
LYDIA. She's right, stop!
ROGER. *(Overlap.)* You just get us to question ourselves to the point of stupefaction. We got caught off guard. And that's never going to happen again, I can tell you that.
TERENCE. Yet another moment of sophisticated American analysis.
ROGER. Fuck you, asshole.
TERENCE. Fuck you, you fucking Nazi moron!
ROGER. Fuck you, faggot!
SUZIE. Roger—
LYDIA. *(To JEFF.)* He's hurt!
JEFF. Am I supposed to care about that?
KHALID. Stop it, stop it! In my moment of shame can you not see, can you not learn—my world is disintegrating, my people cannot speak to each other, we are descending into utter hell and this is all you can do for us, for yourselves—for the earth, think of the earth!

(The others stop, silenced for a moment.)

JULIA. Well, I'm going to take that gag out of his mouth. I concede he might need to be restrained. But I will not see him gagged.

(She pushes by JEFF, leans over MOHAMMED and takes the gag out of his mouth. Immediately:)

MOHAMMED. Everything you do to silence the Arab community. America's corrupt global policy. Silence the Arabs! You take our oil, you take our wealth, but you will not listen!
LYDIA. Listen, Mohammed—you should probably try not to provoke people right now.
MOHAMMED. American women are whores.
LYDIA. Okay. My mistake. Carry on.
MOHAMMED. Three thousands of your people die in the World Trade Center, do you know how many you've killed in Afghanistan and Iraq, how many you abandoned to die under your trade embargoes in Pakistan?
ROGER. You tested nuclear weapons!
MOHAMMED. You invented nuclear weapons! You come into our lands only to murder us, how many Iraqi children murdered in their homes, so you can have your oil—
ROGER. Listen to me. Your leaders are conning you.
MOHAMMED. *(Overlap.)* You are the bully of the world—
ROGER. Listen to me, will you just—
JULIA. Stop, it's going nowhere—
MOHAMMED. *(Overlap.)* We suffer and die under your war machine everywhere, you only export war to our peoples in Palestine, in Afghanistan, in Iraq, everywhere, everywhere you kill us—
ROGER. By making America the perpetual target of your troubles, you allow your leaders to deceive you and steal from you ... ahh forget it!
MOHAMMED. *(Overlap.)* And your media distorts and lies about our world, and makes us look like simpleminded masses, so you

can continue to murder us without feeling—

ROGER. My blood pressure is soaring—I'm not listening!!

MOHAMMED. You know this to be true!!!!

JEFF. *(Yelling, sudden.)* But that doesn't give you the right to come into our country and kill us—

MOHAMMED. Nor you! Nor you!

JEFF. You fucking—you fucking— *(JEFF hauls off, about to slug the helpless MOHAMMED in the face. After a moment, JEFF shakes his head. Vulnerable:)* I'm sorry. I can't…. It's too…. I can't, Suzie….

SUZIE. It's all right, dear.

KHALID. *(To MOHAMMED.)* Who are you speaking to? Do you think you are speaking to me? To these people, you have already said you have nothing but contempt for them, you want to destroy them. So I ask you, are you speaking to me?

MOHAMMED. I speak for the Arabs.

KHALID. You are alienating the group you are fighting for. This is what I want to ask you. If you get to the place that you want, the land of milk and honey, how will you be able to forget how you got there? Can you kill and slaughter your way into heaven? And if you get in, then, that way, do you really belong there?

MOHAMMED. I do what is asked of me.

KHALID. I ask you something. I ask you to answer me, as a fellow Arab. I ask you to explain. Because I tell you, we can find peace through negotiation, with the other peoples of the world, our neighbors, or we can find peace by killing off all our enemies. Both will bring peace. *(Beat.)* But which is peace?

MOHAMMED. They will give us nothing, if we give them peace! The only power we have is to deny them peace, to be the destroyers of the universe. It is the only power they have left us.

JULIA. Oh my god—

MOHAMMED. You know this to be true!

KHALID. No, my friend. I do not accept that. Anta jooan?

[Translation: Are you hungry?]
MOHAMMED. Kul shaebna jooan. [Translation: All of our people are hungry.]
KHALID. Lehake lazim takul. [Translation: Then you must eat.]

(He goes to him and brings him to the table, finds a seat for him.)

JULIA. What, what did you say to him?
KHALID. I asked him if he is hungry. He says yes. We must feed him, Suzie.
SUZIE. *Une place ala table maintenent*!
TERENCE. Quite right. Can't have him critiquing our manners, on top of everything else he has to complain about.
ROGER. Hey. Call me crazy, but I don't actually want to have dinner with a destroyer of the universe!
JULIA. Is there an extra plate?
SUZIE. Of course. *Mais oui*!!

(She clears a place for him.)

JULIA. We'll have to untie his hands.
ROGER. No.
JULIA. How else will he be able to eat?
ROGER. I don't give a shit if he eats or not.
MOHAMMED. Yes, this is American policy toward the Arab world. Let them starve.
SUZIE. It's not American policy, sweetie, it's just old RogPog being a sourpussy again. Don't forget the relish, and Lydia, dear, could you give Mr. Mohammed a half-dollop of salad, just so there's something dynamic on the plate?
LYDIA. Fine, but I'm not giving up my crackers.

(Plates are passed.)

JULIA. I'm going to untie your hands now.
ROGER. I don't think that's a good idea.

(MOHAMMED looks at her. She unties his hands. All are watching, alert. He reaches over and picks up a fork. For a moment, it looks like a weapon in his hand, then he starts to eat with it. All visibly relax, watch him eat for a moment.)

MOHAMMED. This is very good.
SUZIE. And, it's been blessed by a Rabbi. *(Everyone is shocked.)* I mean, oh god, I mean, not the Rabbi, it's whatsitcalled, the the the Muslim version of of of kosher—
MOHAMMED. Halel.
SUZIE. Halel! Halel! Of course, Halel!
TERENCE. Wine?
SUZIE. I'll have some!
TERENCE. Wine? *(Offers it to MOHAMMED, who declines.)* Quite right, here's to moral integrity.

(TERENCE drinks.)

MOHAMMED. So much food. This would be enough to feed my children for a week.
JEFF. You have children?
MOHAMMED. Two little girls. Beautiful. Like their mother.
ROGER. What a liar.
LYDIA. Why would he lie about that?
ROGER. They're pathological liars!
JEFF. I have three myself. Two boys and a little girl. They're all great, but she's, she's … my heart. I sure wish I could see them grow up.
JULIA. *(Cautious, confused.)* You're not going to watch them grow up?
JEFF. No.

JULIA. Why, what happened?
SUZIE. I'm sorry. Didn't I tell you? He's dead, dear.
JULIA. He's dead?
JEFF. Yeah.
JULIA. You died?
JEFF. Uh-huh.
JULIA. In the—I had no idea!
TERENCE. I'm sorry, I'm a tad fuzzy. Did you just say—
SUZIE. Yes, yes, he's dead! I told you—
TERENCE. Suzie, I think I'd remember that.
ROGER. I didn't know.
SUZIE. I told someone, didn't I? *(They all stare at her in shock.)* Oh dear. I'm sorry. There's so much to remember, putting together the perfect dinner party, the details all start to run together—
TERENCE. Details?
SUZIE. I'm sorry, I said I'm sorry!
JEFF. Look, it's okay. Could I have more of the lamb, even though we already had salad?
SUZIE. Of course dear. Absolutely.

(She finds it for him.)

TERENCE. Is anyone else here dead?
SUZIE. I don't think so.
TERENCE. Suzie, your reliability has already been shot on this matter.
MOHAMMED. I'm dead.
KHALID. Are we all dead? Is that what that pit's all about?
JULIA. Oh, dear.
LYDIA. Come on!
ROGER. No no, come on. There was no tunnel, no light!
MOHAMMED. No virgins.
KHALID. The pit, the air, the fire—are we in hell?

SUZIE. Let's just say we're in a hellish situation. But we're not dead! We're too lively to be dead! Mohammed, would you like more?

MOHAMMED. Yes of course.

KHALID. I feel myself ... heartbroken.

SUZIE. No, no darling really, everything is fine! We're all fine!

KHALID. Nothing is fine! Is this the end? Is this all we have made of ourselves? Look at the world! We have created a world in which only the most amoral behavior, whatever makes a dollar, whatever sells, whatever tastes good, whatever feels good, that is what is promoted! And that, that is the logic of the pornographer! It is the logic of the child pornographer, who abandons all human feeling, who corrupts the world for his own emptiness! Who destroys the children—

MOHAMMED. Yes, yes, that's what we've been saying!

KHALID. No! Look at what you do to the children! What you teach them! The innocence you destroy! You know it is true! And why, why is it when anyone speaks about the power of love it's suddenly an esoteric conversation!?

TERENCE. Well, Khalid—

KHALID. No! No! You who talk so well must learn to listen! We haven't got a lot of time to evolve here! This will be a compassionate universe or it will cease becoming altogether! Let America strive to become the, the size of a true hero, like our friend the firefighter! Let her assistance be brave and supernatural!

TERENCE. And how would you go about doing this?

KHALID. By feeding everyone!

LYDIA. With what?

KHALID. With food! The fear we feel is because we do not see where or how or if a new world will be born!

ROGER. Look, you're not providing us with any viable plan of action, man!

KHALID. *(Hitting table.)* The action of love, my silly friend, the action of love! Forgive me, you're not silly. Not entirely. You're just hungry too, aren't you? Aren't we all? Oh, I'm so depressed. I wish I had no brain, just a heart the size of a giant fruit, then I would feed us all. I would. I would feed us all.

(Pause.)

    JEFF. I'll toast to that.
    KHALID. *(To JEFF.)* You are a very kind man. A brave man, truly. I like you very much. Here's to Jeff.

(They all clink glasses.)

    ROGER. Here. Here.
    LYDIA. Will you tell us what happened?
    JEFF. What, you mean when it happened?
    LYDIA. Yes. When it happened.

(There is a short pause while he figures out what to say.)

    JEFF. It was strange. Going down there? We knew it was bad. You could see, we're in the engine shooting down Flatbush, watching the smoke pouring out of the tower, someone says Jesus God, there's another one. Watching the second plane hit. Running into the buildings. People, falling, raining from the sky. I never saw that before. None of us did. We thought they would hold, the towers, they were like beings, huge old men holding themselves up as long as they could, so that we could save as many, so many pouring down, while we rushed up and up, to the clouds and the wind and the fire. People ask me about life and death, I don't know what to say, they're the same thing to me now. Harm was ... I don't know. I have children. But what else is my life for? We went up and up until the old men couldn't hold anymore, and death came down on all of us. The living and the dead. *(Beat, embarrassed.)* Is there dessert?
    SUZIE. Why yes! Of course! *Ou est ma tete? Ou est ma tete?*

ROGER. Let me give you a hand, doll.

(They go off, to get the desserts.)

TERENCE. Anybody hear the one about the Buddhist monk, the rabbi and the Catholic priest?
JULIA. Oh dear god.
TERENCE. *(Undaunted.)* Well, there was this Buddhist monk, a rabbi and a Catholic priest on the Titanic. The Titanic, I tell you! And it hits—an iceberg. The ship is tossing, it's about to go down! People are falling into the sea as they scramble for the life boats. The life preservers are nowhere to be found! And then the monk, the rabbi and the priest find—three! Three life preservers! But just as they're about to put them on, the monk says, "Wait—what about the children?" The Rabbi, who is in a total panic now, says, "Fuck the children!" And the Catholic priest says, "Is there time?"

(TERRENCE laughs, uproariously amused.)

KHALID. That is a terrible joke, my friend.
TERENCE. My father was a Catholic priest, I can say whatever I want.

(ROGER and SUZIE return with a pile of desserts. They serve them, all round.)

SUZIE. Ta ta ta ta ta ta ta! Sweets for the sweet!
JULIA. That looks amazing!
SUZIE. A cavalcade of brown sugar twills, lemon poppy seed Madelines, hazelnut financiers and, finally, a tri-star strawberry and mascarpone mill-foo-ee-ay. All for you!! All for you!!

(Everyone screams with delight and applauds as she passes the des-

serts around.)

LYDIA. What is this?
SUZIE. *(To LYDIA.)* Napoleon! But it's just named after him. It hasn't got a face. Unless dairy's a problem—?
LYDIA. Oh god I want this!

(She eats voraciously.)

TERENCE. Dessert. My favorite course. Once, at a small *delecteria* at the heel of the boot of Italy I had the most exquisite creme brulee—
SUZIE. It must've been Panna Cotta. They don't do creme brulee over there.
TERENCE. It was sexual, it was sensual. It was mother's milk reconceived, a creamy dream, an addictive consistency with an eighth of an inch of crusty crispy tempered caramel which fractured into shards of naughtiness with the mere "tap tap" of my cool spoon. All senses alert, culled, dedicated and forsworn. This dish quelled all desire, all anxiety, all the world fell to a generous hush all about me.

(They all fall into hush, just like the one he describes. After a moment, there is a sound of helicopters, which grows very loud very quickly.
The sound grows and grows, the chandelier shakes, people look around, frightened; this is far more serious than any interruption so far. There is the sudden sound of a loud explosion, right next door. Everyone reaches out and grabs onto their neighbor for a long moment, as the sound of the helicopters finally fades. They all look at each other, frightened.)

ROGER. *(To LYDIA.)* Sorry. Sorry, dear.
LYDIA. No, it's all right.

KHALID. *(To JULIA.)* Are you all right?
JULIA. Yes, yes—
JEFF. Anyone hurt?
SUZIE. Oh, please, I hope not—
TERENCE. I think everyone's fine, Suzie. Really.
MOHAMMED. Excuse me. Ah—may I have more of that?
SUZIE. Of course, darling.

(She passes it. People laugh, relieved, for a moment.)

LYDIA. *(Subdued.)* This is a good dinner party.
SUZIE. A dinner party is only as good as the guests.
KHALID. Thank you.
TERENCE. Omnium Gatherum. A collection of peculiar souls.
ROGER. Speak for yourself.
LYDIA. Can I have another?
JULIA. You can have mine. I'm watching my weight.
KHALID. But why? You are the most beautiful woman I've ever seen.
JULIA. Why thank you—Khalid—

(He suddenly pulls her into a passionate kiss. Everyone applauds.)

SUZIE. Oh, this really is a perfect dinner party. It's what I yearn for. The way I yearn for wisdom, or grace. *(She suddenly tears up.)* I'm sorry. Oh. It's just, you are all so important to me. And even though it hurts to be so scared, I don't want to forget. I don't want to feel safe anymore. I want to feel just like this. Oh dear, what kind of a host am I, all of a sudden? Carry on! Giddy-up! *Sils vous plait*, please, please! *La Jour de Fete est arrivez*!!

(Music comes up, something light, tuneful, fun, with haunting undertones. As they all look around, surprised, paper confetti begins to

waft from the ceiling in a gentle, multi-colored snowfall.)

ROGER. Come on, Suzie....

(He takes her hand. They start to dance. TERENCE lights up. LYDIA takes a moment to reflect on her stomach. KHALID and JULIA kiss. MOHAMMED eats, hungry. The music continues. In the distance, the rumble of faint explosions can be heard. The explosions get closer and closer until one loud, terrifying explosion bathes the room in a sudden white light.
Blackout.)

Lightning Source UK Ltd.
Milton Keynes UK
UKHW011329080223
416610UK00017B/2332

9 780573 629594